palette knife and continue painting. You can even scrape down an entire wet canvas for a fresh start! Oil paint truly allows for endless trial and error. While watercolor's unpredictable nature is part of its charm, not everyone wants to relinquish so much control. Oil painting is a fantastic medium for those who want their paint to stay precisely where they put it!

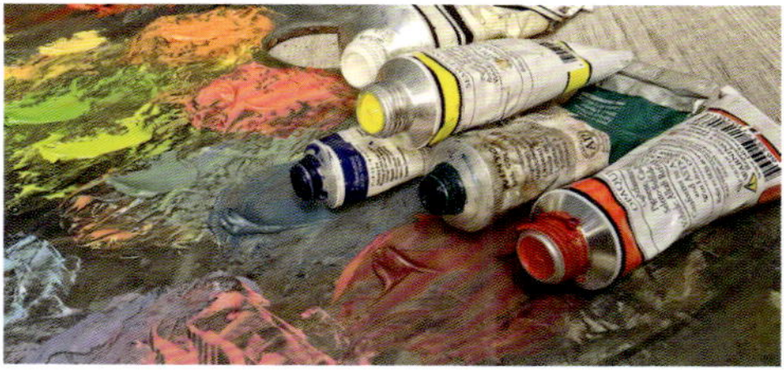

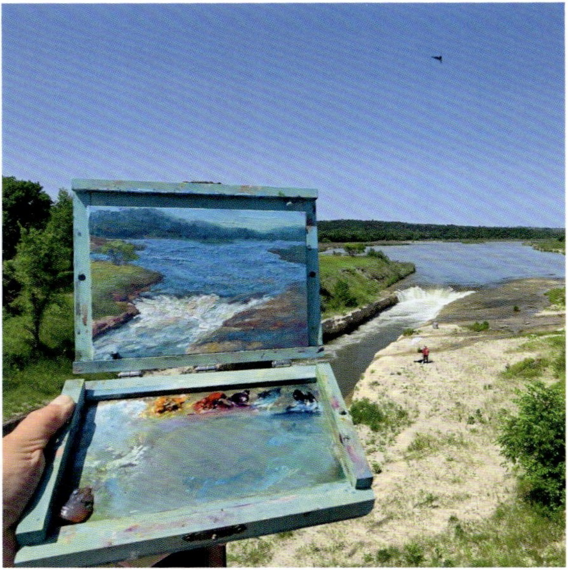

Oil painting is a versatile medium for studio paintings as well as outdoor studies. Please see my other book *Plein Air Painting: Pocket Guide* for more information on painting outside.

OIL PAINTING 101

POCKET GUIDE

TABLE OF CONTENTS

01 INTRODUCTION: DEBUNKING OIL PAINTING MYTHS

Oil painting has transcended the centuries and remains one of the most popular mediums for artistic expression, yet it can seem intimidating. Oil paint is versatile, and the painter has the flexibility to create a personalized workflow to suit their preferences.

Complicated and toxic? Not so much: Frankly, painting with oils can be as simple or complicated as the artist prefers. You can complete an oil painting in one sitting (alla prima technique), or you can work on it for weeks or years with indirect painting techniques. Alla prima (wet into wet) allows you to finish a painting more quickly, but it still requires an intentional method of application. Alla prima technique is what will be demonstrated in this guide.

A common misconception among beginners is that oil paint is inherently toxic, leading many to opt for watercolors or acrylics. The truth is you can entirely avoid toxins in oil painting! The key is to steer clear of solvents (like turpentine and odorless mineral spirits) and to educate yourself about your pigments. Here's a crucial point: a pigment that's toxic in oil paint is also toxic in watercolor, acrylic, or any other medium.

So, learning to identify and handle pigments responsibly is essential, no matter which paint medium you choose. Here are some other pros to using oil paints:

Easier to maintain brushes than acrylic painting: I can speak from personal experience on this one! Acrylic paint, being a plastic, becomes a permanent fixture on your brush bristles once it hardens—a lost cause. But with oil paint? I've left thick oil paint to fully harden on brushes for months and still managed to salvage them! Oil paint can be intentionally broken down with an oil-specific soap, even regular dish soap, or surprisingly, even vinegar. Trust me, I've sacrificed far more brushes to acrylics than I ever have to oil painting.

More forgiving and controllable than watercolor: This might surprise you, but oil painting is actually one of the most forgiving paint mediums out there. Watercolor, as a transparent and staining medium, offers very few chances for correction. Once it's on the paper, you can only add more transparent layers, or resort to an opaque medium like gouache, which fundamentally changes its uniquely transparent quality. And while you can soak paper for hours to lift some stain, you'll never truly get back to pristine white paper.

With oils, corrections are straightforward. You can simply apply opaque paint over an error (especially if it has dried). If the paint is still wet, you can scrape just the mistake off with a

02 MATERIALS & TOOLS

PAINTS: RECOMMENDED BRANDS AND AVOIDING TOXIC PIGMENTS

I personally use a diverse range of paint brands for oil painting. For beginners, Winsor & Newton (Winton) and Gamblin (Gamblin 1980) are excellent choices. They offer entry-level paints that are both affordable and surprisingly good quality. I still regularly use Winton paints for toning canvases and for plein air painting. I highly recommend picking one brand and starting with small 37mL tubes to build a limited primary palette—we'll talk more about why that's so beneficial in the "Working with a Limited Palette" section.

To ensure your pigments are non-toxic, make it a habit to avoid tubes of paint containing cadmium, cobalt, lead, chrome, and mercury. Common culprits include cadmium yellows and reds, cobalt blues, greens, and violets, Naples Yellow (which contains lead), and true vermillion (which contains mercury). Your first clue that a pigment might be toxic is its price tag! Cadmiums, cobalts, and lead white pigments are notoriously expensive, so avoiding them protects both your health and your wallet. That said, it's not strictly necessary to completely avoid these pigments as long as you take sensible precautions, like wearing gloves and preventing exposure to your face and skin.

UNDERSTANDING PAINT PROPERTIES

There are a few key properties of oil paint you should be aware of.

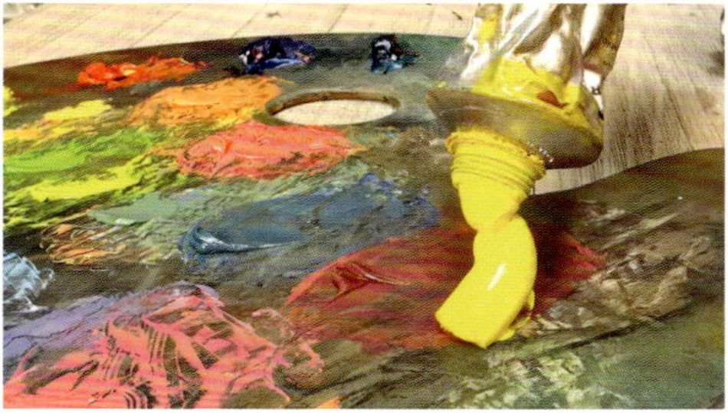

Lightfastness: This describes a pigment's resistance to fading when exposed to ultraviolet (UV) light. For optimal longevity, look for paints rated AA, A, or I. Be aware that some popular colors, like Alizarin Crimson, are known to be "fugitive" (not lightfast) and can fade over time, even from UV light coming through windows.

Single-pigment vs. "hues": You might see names like "Cobalt Teal Hue" or "Cadmium-free Red." This indicates that the tube isn't a single pigment, but rather a mixture of other (often less expensive and typically non-toxic) pigments designed to mimic the properties of a more costly or toxic pigment. "Hues" are a fantastic, safer option to consider.

Transparency vs. opacity: Some pigments are naturally transparent (allowing light to pass through), while others are opaque (light-blocking). Finely ground pigments suspended in more oil tend to be more transparent, while more coarsely ground pigments with less oil are more opaque. Transparent paint is wonderful for subtle glazes, whereas opaque paint lends itself beautifully to alla prima (wet-into-wet) techniques. Both are valuable, and knowing how to use them enhances your process.

Oxidation (drying): Oil paintings don't actually "dry" because there is no water to evaporate. Rather, they cure or harden. This is a chemical process where the paint molecules interact with oxygen in the environment. This curing process is vital and continues long after a painting is "dry to the touch." This is why we never place oil paintings under glass—they need to be exposed to oxygen to cure properly over time.

Brushes (types, sizes, and care tips): Bristle brushes are the workhorses of oil painting. You can find them made from natural hog hair or synthetics. The defining characteristic of a good bristle brush is its somewhat rigid and thick bristles. This stiffness is perfect for pushing thick oil paint around the canvas or board without needing to thin it down with solvents or mediums. Some artists exclusively use bristle brushes, loving the rich, painterly textured strokes they create. Others use them for the initial layers, then switch to softer brushes for finer details and top layers.

Soft brushes, too, can be natural (like sable, which is typically more expensive) or synthetic (like taklon). These aren't ideal for the very first stages of painting but excel in the final layer or two. They're perfect for applying delicate glazes and precise details, especially with paint that might be slightly thinned with a medium.

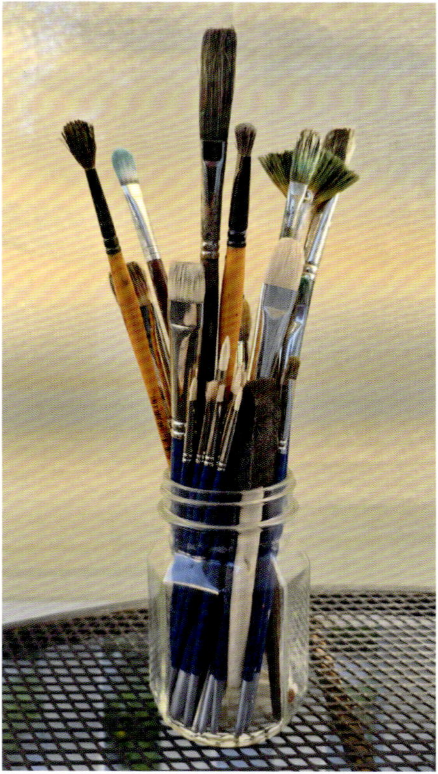

Palettes (wood vs. glass vs. disposable paper): The market offers a wide variety of palettes. Many artists swear by a glass palette because it's relatively easy to clean. You can also place a neutral middle-gray paper underneath it, which really helps in accurately judging the values of your color mixes. Wood palettes have their own charm: they offer a pleasant middle tone (though warmer than a neutral gray), are more portable and less prone to breaking, and provide a tactile experience many painters prefer (think of the soft clinking of a palette knife on wood compared to glass).

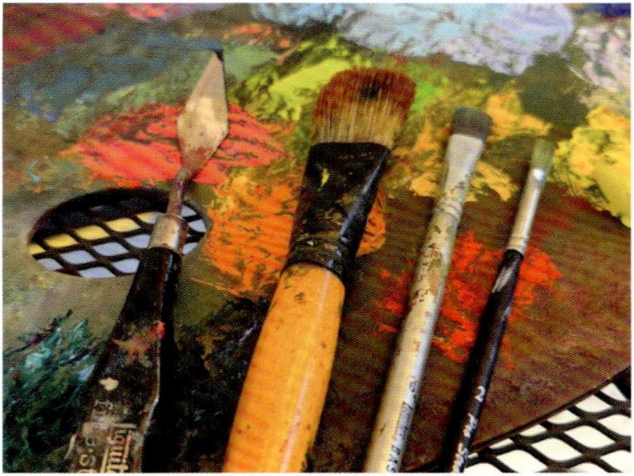

How clean you keep your palette is entirely up to you—there are successful artists on both ends of the spectrum! If you prefer a pristine palette, scrape it thoroughly after each painting session and rub it with linseed oil to help prevent permanent staining (some pigments will stain, especially wood).

Canvas and supports: The substrate you choose for your oil painting will depend on the amount of rigidity and texture you prefer for your surface. Let's explore some common options:

Stretched canvas (or linen): This is what most people picture—a canvas stretched taut over a wooden frame. It should feel firm but will always have a slight give. You can even see light through it if it's properly primed. "Gallery wrapped" canvases are deep-sided, allowing you to paint the edges and hang them without a frame. Canvas has a coarser weave than linen, which is usually more expensive. While popular, be aware that stretched canvas can sag due to environmental shifts (temperature, humidity), eventually needing re-stretching. They are also more prone to tears or punctures since there's no firm backing.

Canvas (or linen) panel: Here, canvas or linen fabric is glued to a firm backing, often cardboard or wood. This is a fantastic option, offering the familiar canvas texture with added durability. Panels are low-profile (typically 1/8th-inch thick) but can be "cradled" onto a deeper wood frame for a more substantial look. You won't worry about warping with a panel, and they're incredibly easy to transport for plein air painting. Prices are reasonable, especially if you buy in bulk, though linen panels or oil-primed panels will cost more.

Gesso board: This is a wood substrate primed with gesso (an acrylic-based primer, perfectly compatible with oil paint). Gesso board can be pricier but offers a much smoother surface than canvas or linen, which artists often prefer for sharper edges or very fine detail. Like panels, gesso board is rigid, won't warp, and is resilient to damage. It can be framed or hung cradled.

Masonite/hardboard: For the DIY enthusiast, making your own gesso board from Masonite (also known as hardboard) is incredibly easy and cost-effective! You can buy large sheets at hardware stores, and many will even cut them down to painting-sized panels for you. Simply sand off the glossy coating and apply your own gesso or oil primer. A full 4×8-foot sheet of Masonite can yield dozens of 9×12-inch panels for a fraction of the cost of pre-made ones! Once primed, you'll have a wonderfully firm, smooth surface that resists warping (unless you're working on a very large piece with thin board—opt for thicker board for large works).

Paper and cardboard: Yes, you absolutely can oil paint on paper or cardboard! There are special papers made for oil painting (like Arches oil paper), or you can prepare your own with thick paper (at least 140lb weight) by simply applying gesso. Paintings on paper can be mounted to a board for presentation. I love using paper and cardboard for quick studies because they stack easily, don't take up much space, and are incredibly cheap! Keep in mind that even when primed, paper and cardboard tend to be more absorbent, so your paintings might dry with a more matte finish as the oils sink in more.

SIZING AND PRIMING

You'll find most substrates already primed with either gesso (acrylic) or an oil primer. Some artists have a strong preference, but gesso is typically less expensive.

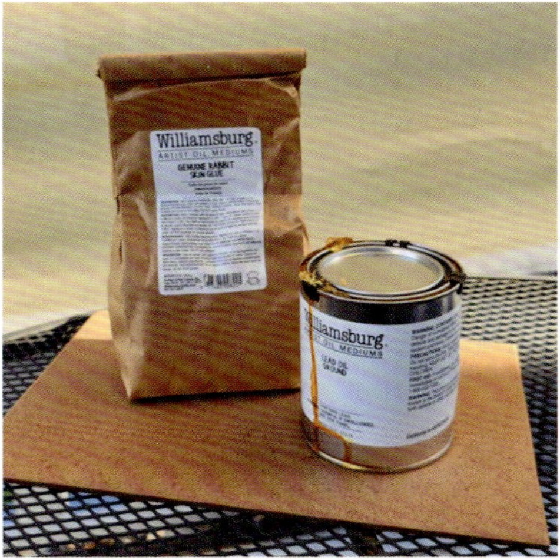

If you plan to make your own substrate, you need to understand sizing. Especially for porous materials like wood, canvas, or linen, you'll need to "size" the material *before* you prime it. Sizing helps maintain the integrity of the fabric by preventing it from absorbing the oils from your paint, which can cause the material to deteriorate over time. While gesso offers good protection, if you plan to use an oil primer, you'll definitely need to apply a dedicated sizing like Rabbit Skin Glue or Polyvinyl Acetate (PVA).

MEDIUMS

First, let me emphasize that using any medium is completely optional. You can absolutely create beautiful oil paintings without them. For those who do choose to use mediums, it's crucial to use them sparingly and for very specific applications. Using too much medium, or using it inconsistently, can actually weaken the integrity of your paint film or interfere with its crucial oxidation (drying/curing) process.

Linseed or walnut oil: Natural, traditional, and slow-drying linseed oil is an organic medium derived from flax seeds and is the binding agent for most tubes of oil paint. Walnut oil is similar, though less common, and has the advantage of being less prone to yellowing over time.

It's generally best to use linseed or walnut oil in the latter stages of your painting process. Using it too early, especially if you're building multiple layers, can prevent the bottom layers from fully oxidizing (unless you allow them to cure completely before adding subsequent layers). Oil mediums are considered "fat," and it's vital to adhere to the "fat over lean" principle in oil painting: bottom layers should contain little to no additional fats (oils), while subsequent layers may contain progressively more.

A common beginner mistake is to try and use oil mediums in place of solvents for the very first, thin layer of paint. Solvents are "lean" and make paint dry faster, making them suitable for early layers. Adding more oil, however, should typically only occur in the final one or two layers of a multi-layered painting.

Use just enough oil medium to slightly increase the flow and transparency of your paint. Using too much can damage the paint's integrity, leading to brittleness, wrinkling, or excessive yellowing as the paint oxidizes over time. Keep in mind that oils with no quick-dry additives will slow down the drying process, so layers containing them will take longer to become dry to the touch.

Alkyd mediums like Liquin: Another very popular oil painting medium is alkyd, which comes in various forms (e.g., Winsor & Newton's Liquin line and Gamblin's Galkyd line). The primary reason artists use alkyd mediums is to accelerate the curing process of their oil paintings. You can find alkyd mediums that increase flow and transparency, much like linseed oil, but with a significantly faster drying time. There are also "impasto" alkyd mediums that help maintain the thickness of your oil paint while speeding up the setup. Alkyds are synthetic (unlike organic linseed/walnut oils) and are generally less prone to yellowing.

A great advantage of alkyds is that you can use them in the early stages of painting—for instance, creating a thin underpainting that dries quickly (sometimes in as little as 24 hours), allowing you to apply additional layers or glazes sooner. You can then continue using alkyd mediums in all subsequent layers. What you *must* avoid is using alkyds *only* in the latter stages of a painting, as this can seal off earlier layers and prevent them from fully curing, risking deterioration over time. The general guideline is either use alkyds consistently from the beginning, or don't use them at all.

Most alkyd mediums do contain solvents and will produce a low level of fumes. Therefore, it's wise to avoid direct contact with alkyds and always use them in a well-ventilated area.

03 WORKING SAFELY WITH OR WITHOUT SOLVENTS

I tend to avoid using solvents. While solvents have long been popular for thinning paint in initial layers and for cleaning brushes, they are, frankly, the only inherently toxic material in oil painting. All solvents (like turpentine, mineral spirits, and spike lavender oil) produce fumes that are irritating and potentially damaging to humans. Even "odorless" mineral spirits produce fumes and can be damaging to human tissue (eyes, mouth, skin).

If you absolutely must use solvents, you can mitigate the risks by taking serious precautions:

Keep containers airtight: Only open your solvent container just before you're about to dip your brush and close it immediately after. Glass or steel containers are best.

Work in a well-ventilated space: Open windows, use fans, or ideally, work outdoors.

Avoid skin contact: Wear gloves and never touch your face with solvent-laden hands.

Keep away from food and water.

Proper disposal: Look up local resources for hazardous waste disposal. I personally keep a large glass jar for dirty solvent liquid, storing it outside until it's time for proper disposal.

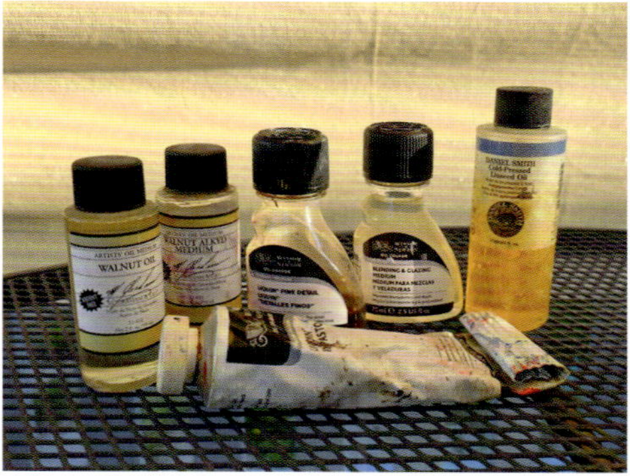

BRUSH CLEANING WITHOUT SOLVENTS

Rinsing in linseed oil (daily cleaning): I used to believe there was no way to properly clean oil painting brushes without solvents. But guess what? You can actually clean your brushes *better* with just linseed (or walnut) oil! I keep a small bottle of linseed oil handy. When I finish painting, I use a thick paper towel to remove as much excess paint from the bristles as possible. Then, I dip the bristles into the linseed oil and blot it onto the towel. I repeat this oil-blot process until my brush is sufficiently clean (I never aim for 100% spotless, as a little residual pigment is fine). This method not only cleans but also conditions your brushes, significantly increasing their longevity—solvents, in contrast, will damage brushes over time.

Deep cleaning with dish soap and water: For a truly deep clean, use either an oil-specific soap or even regular dish soap to clean your brushes once a week or even once a month. The soap effectively breaks down the oils, leaving your brushes thoroughly clean.

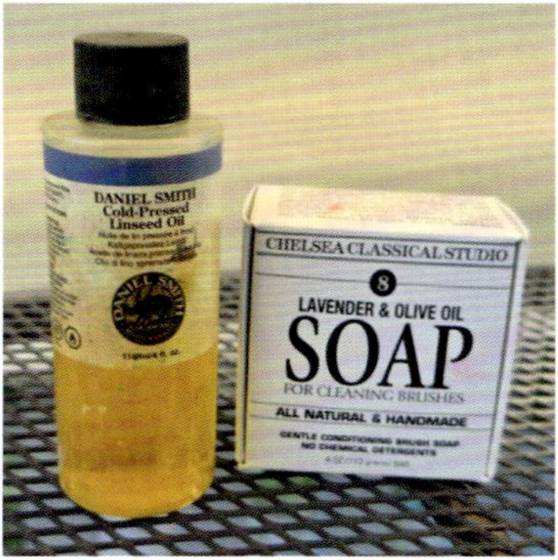

TIP: If you accidentally get oil paint on clothing or carpet, a bit of dish soap and water will work wonders to remove it!

04 UNDERSTANDING YOUR PAINTS & MIXING COLORS

WORKING WITH A LIMITED PALETTE

As a beginner, intentionally limiting the number of colors on your palette offers multiple benefits:

Cost-effectiveness: With fewer tubes to buy, you can invest in higher-quality paints, which makes a big difference in how they handle.

Intimate familiarity: You'll become deeply familiar with the unique properties of each of your colors. Not all yellows are created equal, and colors that look similar are often not interchangeable. A limited palette forces you to truly get to know each one.

Reduces decision paralysis: Too many choices can lead to overthinking and "decision paralysis" before you even start painting. A smaller palette simplifies things, allowing you to focus on the act of painting.

Unlocks mixing mastery: There's no single "best" palette and getting hung up on using the exact same colors as your favorite artists can be a distraction. By starting with a few colors, you'll unlock the incredibly wide array of colors you can achieve through almost infinite mixing proportions. You can always add new colors one by one as you explore.

RECOMMENDED SIX-COLOR LIMITED PALETTE

Here's a fantastic starting point for a limited palette. Feel free to swap out the blue if you already have one you prefer!

Titanium White: The most opaque and cool white.

Raw Umber: A semi-transparent earth pigment that dries relatively quickly. It's fantastic for toning down overly vibrant mixes and is very popular for toning your painting surface and doing an underpainting.

Ultramarine Blue: A dark, transparent blue that leans slightly towards violet on the color wheel. It creates beautiful, earthy greens when mixed with most yellows. While it's difficult to get a bright "turquoise" with this color alone, it's a standard, versatile blue.

Azo Yellow: A vibrant, semi-transparent, sunshine-like yellow. It's quite intense, so a little goes a long way.

Naphthol Red: An intense, semi-opaque red. It's a wonderful, non-toxic alternative to Cadmium Red, offering similar vibrancy without the toxicity.

Phthalo or Viridian Green: Be warned, this is a VERY strong and transparent color! You absolutely must learn to wield it, as it will easily dominate your mixes. It's often too unnatural to use straight as a "green" in its own right. However, with this recommended palette, a tiny touch of Phthalo Green mixed with Ultramarine Blue is your best bet for achieving a nice turquoise, which can be crucial for water scenes or painting fabrics. It's also excellent for toning down reds.

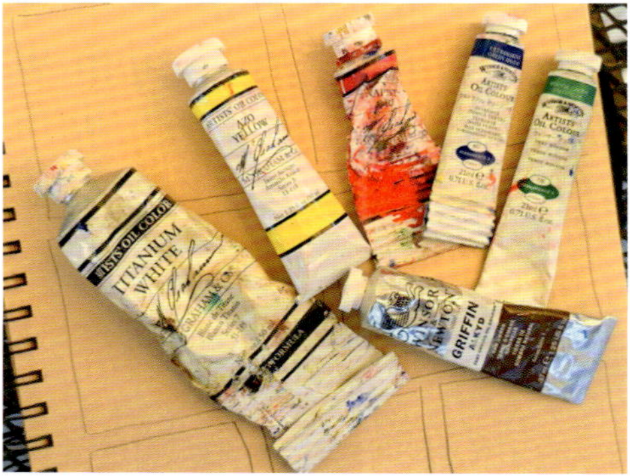

MIXING BASICS: HOW TO CREATE A FULL RANGE OF COLORS FROM A LIMITED PALETTE

Once you have your chosen limited palette, dedicate some time to truly understanding its potential. Start by creating a color wheel with your chosen pigments. Then, challenge yourself to create a color swatch chart where you systematically mix every color with every other color on your palette—this will reveal combinations you might not explore otherwise.

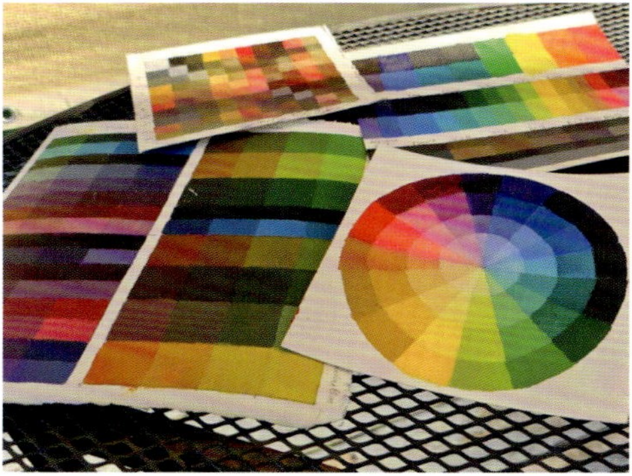

Next, I highly recommend a fun exercise: visit your local hardware store, grab some paint sample cards, and then use only your limited palette to try and match those sample colors.

This will push you to mix colors in ways that aren't immediately obvious. For example, you'll discover that achieving a nuanced sage green requires more than just blue, yellow, and white.

Finally, take your paints outdoors for some plein air sessions to observe natural light. Practice what I call "color notes." This involves simply mixing the colors you observe in nature and applying them directly onto your canvas without trying to paint "objects" or feeling pressure to create a finished "painting." The result is often a very colorful, almost abstract composition, and you might even find you like these color notes enough to hang them!

UNDERSTANDING WARM VS. COOL VERSIONS OF COLORS

This aspect of color theory can get quite "in the weeds," which is beyond the scope of this beginner's guide. However, as you begin, try doing a few studies where you intentionally use a "cool" color (like blue) for your dark values, and a "warm" color (like red) for your lighter values. Your middle values will then be a combination of these cool and warm colors. Of course, you can also use your white to lighten values as needed. This simple exercise will start building your intuition for color temperature.

WHY PRE-MIXING CAN MAKE PAINTING EASIER

One of my favorite ways to warm up before diving into a new painting is to pre-mix several colors and place small piles on my palette. I often do this when painting from a photo. I'll analyze the photo to estimate the range of colors and values I think I'll need. This approach helps me stick to a more limited color scheme than what I see in the photo or simply provides a convenient starting point from which I can easily achieve even more nuanced mixes as I go. Doing this makes the actual painting process run much smoother, as I'm not constantly mixing new colors and getting pulled out of my "flow state." It's also a great mental exercise that helps you translate your artistic thoughts into tangible colors before your brush even touches the canvas.

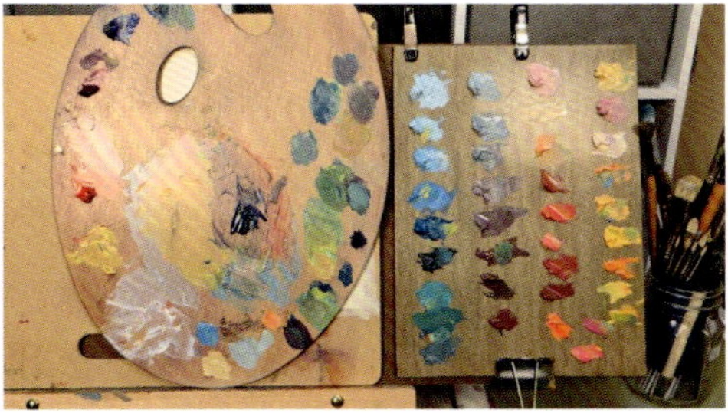

LEARNING WHERE AND HOW TO USE HARD VS. SOFT EDGES

A great exercise is painting a simple sphere with a basic background. The subtle value changes within the sphere will require soft edges (values that shift gradually, perhaps with a little blending), while the edge that defines the sphere against the background will be harder (a crisp, clean transition). Many beginner painters tend to over-blend, which can make a painting feel like a "blob" and flatten forms. Practice mixing values that evolve subtly and use that gradual shift in values to create softness, rather than relying solely on blending. It's tough to guide a viewer's eye through a painting that's either all soft or all hard. Reserve hard edges for the focal point of your composition to really make it stand out.

05 BUILDING A PAINTING STEP-BY-STEP (ALLA PRIMA)

PAINTING FROM REFERENCE

As much as I love painting outdoors, using photos can be a great way to increase your "brush mileage" in the comfort of your own private space.

When considering what photo to use, don't be too picky. Many of my photo references are blurry, amateurish photos taken from my phone. When you snap photos, make a mental note of why that scene caught your eye. If you (like me) are a non-photographer, it's likely that when you look back on your photos you will not feel that same inspiration, but your memory of the moment can help to restore the vision.

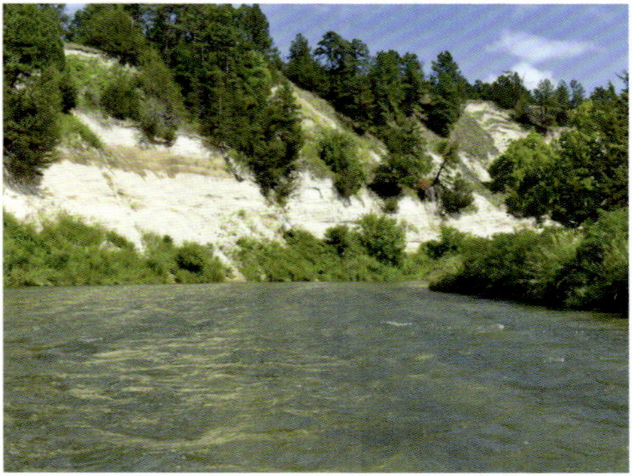

I took this photo years ago while kayaking Nebraska's Niobrara River. I loved the contrast of textures between the sandstone cliffs, water, and the foliage. To me the colors of the photo are not very interesting, and the cliffs are blown out. So, my goal is to take a playful approach to the color and to breathe some life back into the sandstone cliffs.

THE FOUNDATION: SKETCHING AND UNDERPAINTING

Before you even think about laying down thick paint, a solid foundation is key.

Quick composition sketches: Take a few moments to make small thumbnail sketches of your composition. This helps you plan your layout and value masses.

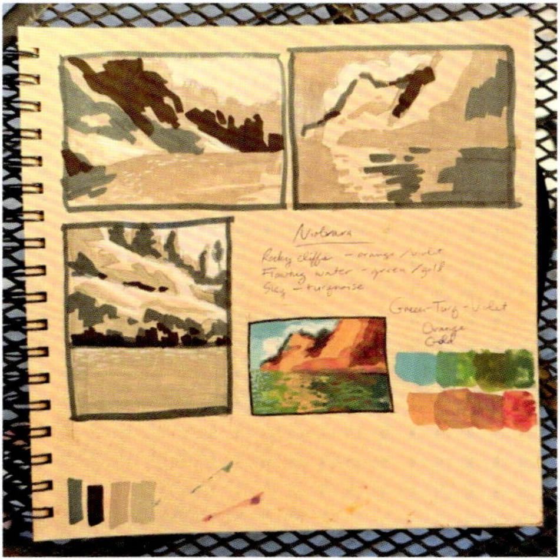

Toning the canvas: Applying a thin, transparent wash of a neutral color (I like to use Raw Umber or I mix my yellow, red, and a bit of blue to get a soft orange) to your canvas helps eliminate the bright white, making it much easier to judge your values and colors accurately.

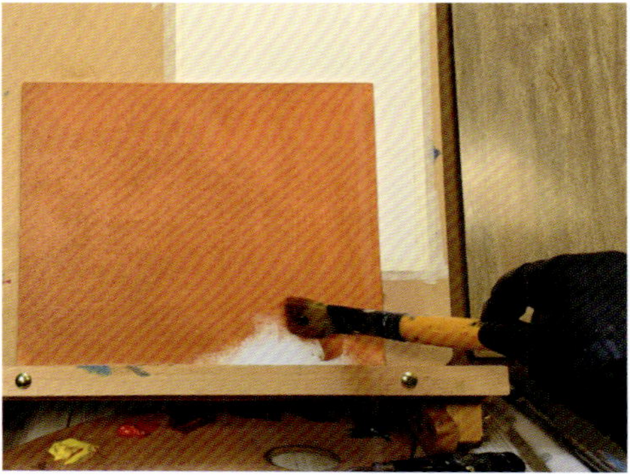

Apply the tone color as thinly as possible. Use a large course brush to scrub the paint into your substrate

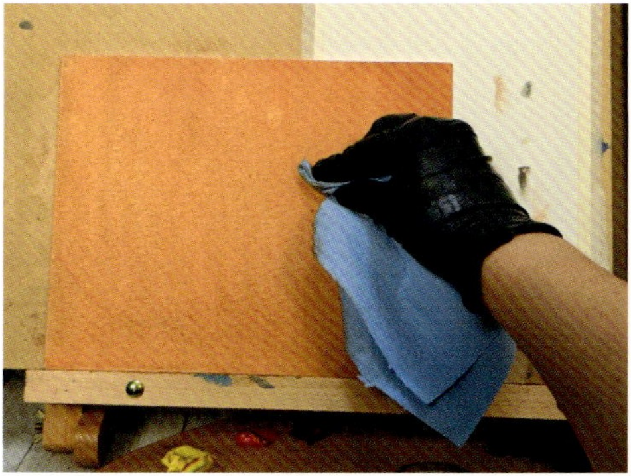

Even when applied thinly, there will be excess paint. Use a paper towel to remove as much excess paint as possible. Or you can let the toned canvas dry. I often tone many canvas panels at once, let them dry, and then grab one when I'm ready to paint.

Pre-mixing colors: This is optional, but I like to use my limited palette of five or six colors to pre-mix a "color scheme" for my painting. In this case, I chose a complementary color scheme of mainly blue-greens and oranges. Once mixed, I use my palette knife to transfer them to a palette that I clip on my easel right next to my painting so I can better judge color and value. I like to organize my pre-mixed piles by hue and value. Doing this means I have a cohesive palette, and I do not have to do as much "color thinking" while I'm in the midst of painting. I never strictly stick to the pre-mixed colors, and some piles won't even get touched. I do not always pre-mix my colors. Especially if painting outdoors (or if I'm just feeling spontaneous) I'll mix on the go.

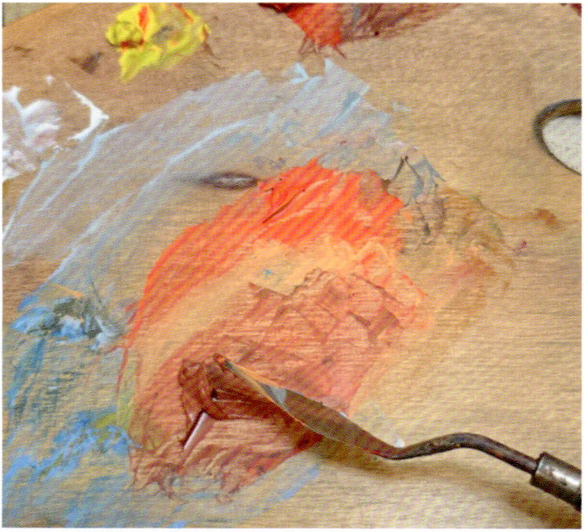

Here you can see that I am preparing to paint by pre-mixing colors from my limited palette.

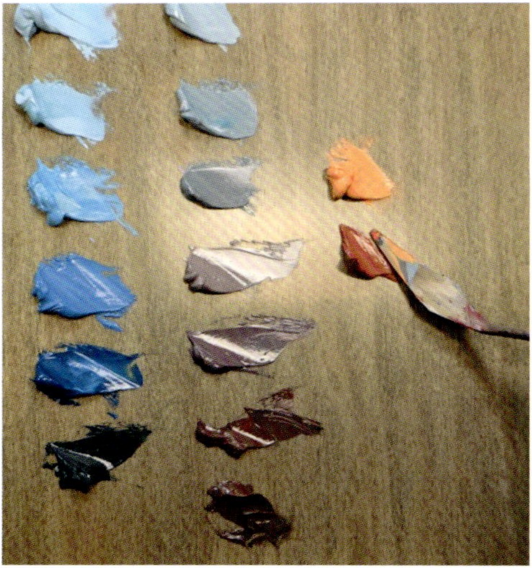

Each pre-mixed color is placed on a rectangular palette clipped onto my easel.

Block-in approach (simple lines and large shapes first): Begin by broadly blocking in the largest shapes and overall value areas of your painting. Don't get caught up in details yet; think in big, simplified forms. Think of your values like a notan—a dark value and the color of your toned canvas.

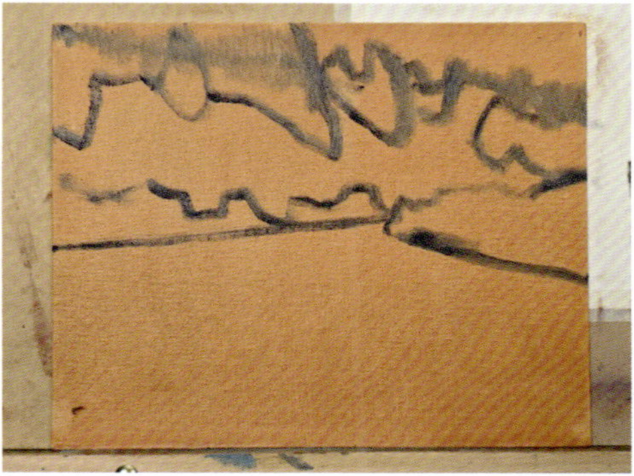

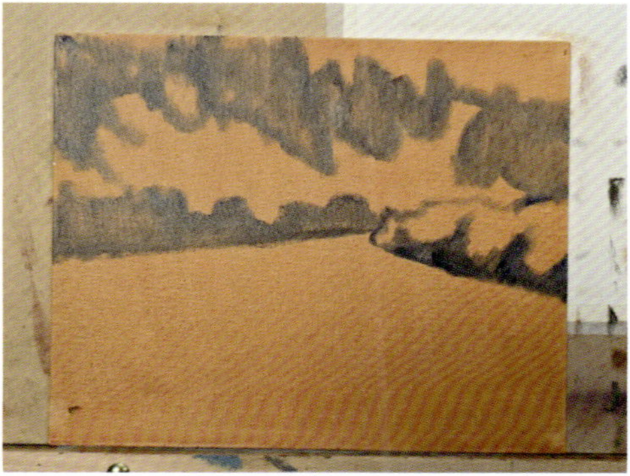

Color block-in: If you are using a photo reference, I recommend making it black and white (at least for this stage) and then just "play" with the initial color block-in. Focus more on value than color. You can see here that I first paint my sky with a thin layer of orange-pink and then I apply a blue over it, allowing some of that pink to show through. I think this is fun and I enjoy the subtle color vibrations.

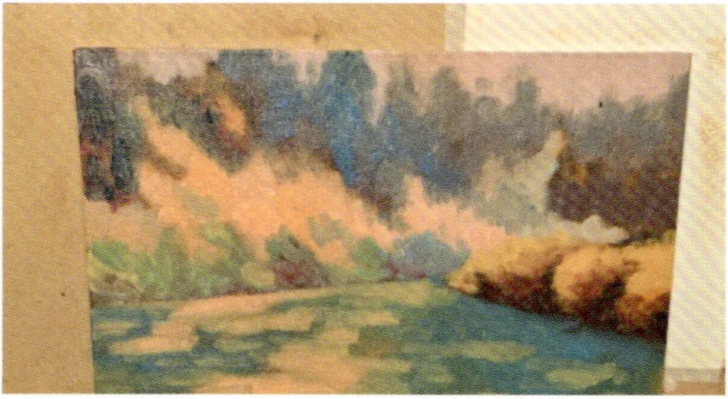

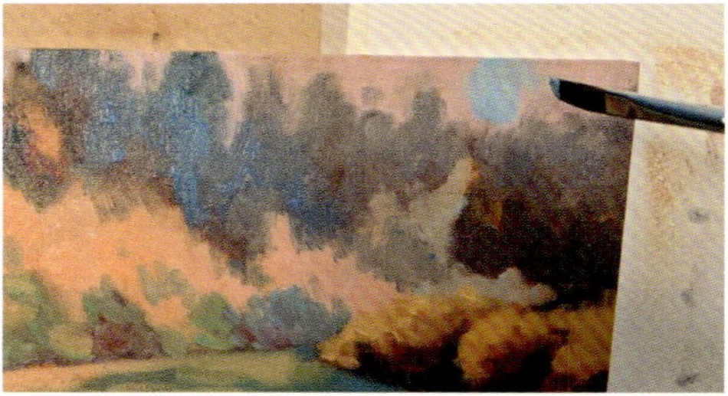

Assess and refine: At least every 30 minutes, make a point to step away from your painting. You'll come back with fresh eyes that will enable you to assess and decide what to focus on next. Tunnel-vision is a fast-track to an overworked painting. Refining your painting will depend on your goal. If your goal is realism, you'll be refining color and value to be as accurate as possible. If your goal is impressionism, you'll be looking for opportunities to play with color, texture, brush strokes and whatever visual elements excite you the most.

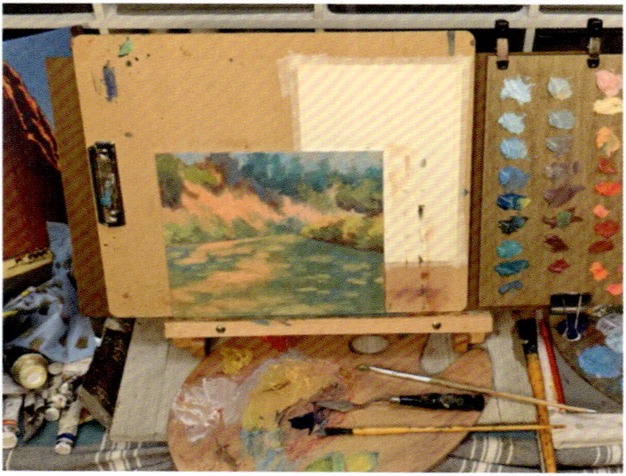

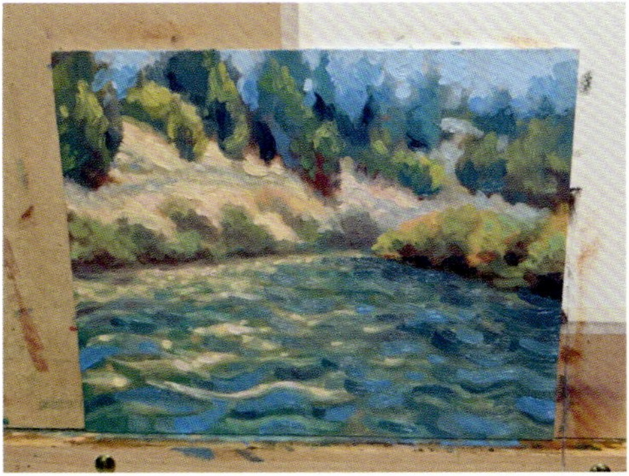

For me, I really wanted to capture all the color and movement in the water. I was drawn to the reflection of the cliffs and the interplay of greens and blues.

I could have left my painting at the previous step, but I decided to push my color scheme and add some of the pink-orange color that I had placed under my sky to the cliffs. I also added orange to some of the middle-ground foliage to further distinguish it from background foliage and trees. These were not colors I observed in my photo reference or from life, rather just my own experimentation.

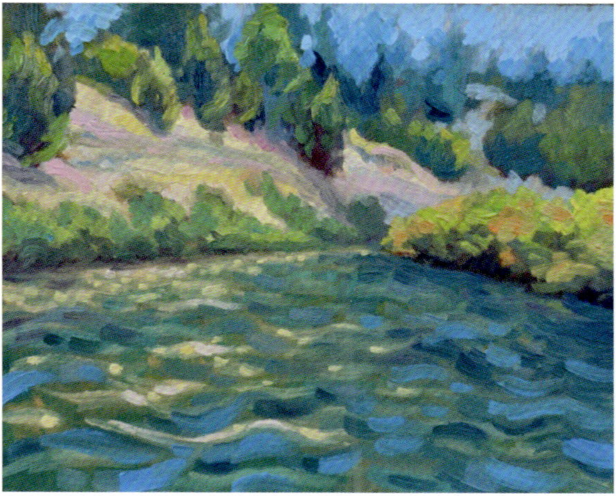

ALLA PRIMA TECHNIQUES

As mentioned, this guide focuses on alla prima—also known as "wet-into-wet" painting. Unlike indirect painting, where layers dry between sessions, alla prima means you finish the painting while the paint is still wet, blending and layering on the spot.

Thin, diluted washes vs. thick, textured strokes: You'll often start with thinner, more diluted washes for initial color statements, then gradually build up to thicker, more textured applications as you refine your forms and add highlights.

The fat-over-lean principle explained simply: This is a crucial concept for oil painting longevity. It means that each subsequent layer of paint must be more flexible than the layer beneath it. In practical terms, "lean" layers (thinner paint, less oil) go down first, and "fat" layers (thicker paint, more oil/medium) go on top. This ensures proper drying and prevents cracking.

Using brushwork to suggest texture: Don't just paint *what* you see, but *how* it feels. Vary your brushstrokes to suggest the texture of trees, the movement of water, or the softness of clouds. Visible brushstrokes are part of the beauty of oil painting!

Using a palette knife to apply paint: A palette knife isn't just for mixing! It's fantastic for applying thick, impasto paint, creating sharp, clean edges, or adding interesting textures. Don't be afraid to experiment with it directly on your canvas.

ADDING LAYERS AND DETAILS

Even in alla prima, there's a sense of building and refining.

Gradual refinement: Resist the urge to overwork areas too soon. Focus on getting the larger shapes and values right, then slowly refine and add details.

Avoiding muddy colors: While often a problem from overmixing, sometimes "muddy" colors are simply what you need for a more neutral tone. For vibrant colors, ensure your brush is clean between mixes.

Final highlights and finishing touches: Towards the end, add your brightest highlights and crispest details. These are often the "jewels" that make your painting pop!

PROTECTING FINISHED PAINTINGS

Varnish: Varnish is a layer of protection for your finished oil painting. Because oil paint needs to continue to oxidize long after it feels "dry," it should not be placed behind glass. Some varnishes cannot be applied for 6 to 12 months so as not to seal a painting that isn't fully cured. However, Gamvar by Gamblin can be applied as soon as your painting is dry to the touch and allows the paint to continue to cure.

06 TROUBLESHOOTING COMMON PROBLEMS

Paint not adhering to the painting? If you're trying to apply paint and finding it just won't transfer from your brush to your painting, it's likely because you're trying to paint over paint that's too thick and wet. Try these solutions:

Add a medium: A touch of linseed oil can make the new paint more fluid and help it to adhere.

Remove excess: Use a palette knife or a stiff bristle brush to gently scrape off some of the excess wet paint from the surface.

Let it "set up": Sometimes, the best solution is to simply walk away. Allow your painting to sit and "set up" for a day or two before attempting to add more paint.

Change brushes: A softer-haired brush might be able to gently lay paint on top where a rigid bristle brush would just push into the wet paint.

Colors look muddy? First, remember that "muddy" colors are often quite necessary! Most of the colors in a harmonious composition should actually be a bit muted or "toned down," rather than pure, vibrant hues. So, sometimes, what you perceive as "muddy" is actually just a perfectly neutral, intentional mix.

However, if you're aiming for a very vibrant, pure color and struggling, here's what might be happening:

Dirty brush: Your paintbrush bristles might be holding onto pigments from previous mixes. A thorough dip in linseed oil followed by blotting on a paper towel should help clear it out.

Too many pigments: The fewer colors in a mix, the more vibrant the resulting color tends to be. Try to achieve your desired color with as few pigments as possible.

Palette limitations: Your limited palette can indeed be a limiting factor sometimes. For example, if you're trying to mix a bright fuchsia for a flower, but your only red is Naphthol Red (which leans orange), you simply won't achieve that true fuchsia. Fuchsia leans violet, so your instinct might be to mix a blue with your Naphthol Red to get a "violet." Unfortunately, this often produces a very muted, "muddy" violet that looks nothing like fuchsia. While this can be frustrating, it's a valuable learning experience about the properties of the colors on your palette. If you consistently find your limited palette hinders you for a specific subject matter, that's your cue to make an informed decision about adding just one more color to your collection. This slow, deliberate expansion is a much better way to learn than starting with too many pigments and getting overwhelmed.

Drying too slowly? If you know from the start that you need your painting to set up quickly, the solution is simple: use an alkyd medium (like Liquin) consistently throughout the entire process. I recommend adding just a little bit to every single mix you create. What I often do is pre-mix a small amount of Liquin into my Titanium White (which is naturally quite slow-drying) and then have a separate pile of Liquin on my palette to add to all my other mixes.

PLEIN AIR PAINTING

POCKET GUIDE

TABLE OF CONTENTS

won't promise that you'll experience a feeling of Zen the first time (or the tenth time) you go out to paint, but once you get a handle on the basics, you may begin to have the experience of time standing still and feeling completely immersed in the process and the place.

The last benefit I will describe is that plein air painting will not only improve your studio paintings but will likely become a part of your studio practice. In my case, my plein air paintings have a quite different look compared to my studio paintings. I find haphazard brushstrokes and unexpected colors in my plein air paintings, which are absent from my more meticulous studio paintings. So, I will use my plein air painting along with photo references to give my studio paintings more life and vibrancy. It's rare that the composition from a plein air session becomes a studio painting, but I'll still use these small studies to influence the colors and textures of studio paintings. Plein air painting is also where I tend to experiment with alternate color palettes, or to look for opportunities to observe phenomena that photos do not represent well.

01 BENEFITS OF PLEIN AIR PAINTING

A great way to improve your painting skills is to get outside. Plein air painting will teach you how to paint quickly to keep up with changing light conditions, how to mix rich and nuanced color from a limited palette, and you will develop a keen sense of composition (among other practical skills).

You will find that, even when you're not out painting, you are noticing the way the low evening sun hits the tops of trees and makes them look like fire. You'll drive by a frozen lake and start thinking about how the colors reflected on the ice are more diffuse than the colors in the sky. You'll see an old barn and start working out the proportions of each color that you'd mix on your palette for the light and shadow sides of the structure. You'll begin to feel inspired by your everyday surroundings. Plein air painting won't merely change the way you paint; it will change the way you think and the way you see the world around you.

Another common benefit of nurturing the practice of painting outdoors is that it becomes its own form of meditation. I